A Year of Sitting Painfully

R Humphries

Woodettes Publications

Published 2009
by
Woodettes Publications
Houston, Texas, USA

© Woodettes Publications 2009

R Humphries has asserted his right to be identified as the author of this work with all rights reserved including the right of reproduction in whole or in part in any form.

The Library of Congress has catalogued this edition as follows Humphries, R [date]
A Year of Sitting Painfully : a novel by R Humphries
1st Ed.

ISBN 978-0-578-02892-7

www.woodettes.wordpress.com

Author's Note

This is a work of fiction. Names, characters, places and incidents are either the product of the author's imagination or are used fictitiously. Any resemblance to actual events or locales or persons, living or dead, is entirely coincidental.

The stories based at the Woody Back to School Unit are works of adult fiction based upon the real-life fantasy games played by the author, R. Humphries and his wife, the inimitable Jojo.

It is the author's intent to create the Woody Back to School Unit as an imaginative world peopled with a believable cast and set in familiar surroundings within which the readers will become comfortable.

The vernacular used in the stories is a combination of the phraseology derived from writing such as the British penny comics from the nineteen thirties, current language, slang and idioms, and the invented parlance known as Woody Jargon.

As such references to 'beating', 'thrashing', and 'flogging' have no context to the use or avocation of physical violence, with the exception of controlled corporal punishment, against the characters of the stories.

**Dedicated
to
My Beloved Jojo**

Contents

A Rambunctious Return 1
Brats at Risk 5
A Grubby Life 9
Even Brats Have Rights 13
A Flogging for Spanker Spage 17
Ms Lawton's Exit Strategy 21
Hurricane Jojo 25
Never a Truer Word Spoken in Jest 29
Absolutely Creamed 33
Miss Lisa Sutton 37
Miss Bernadette Summers 41
Bogus Whops 45
Low Riders 49
Stalker 53
Highly Recommended 57
Hand Gabbing 61
Nixdown and Penelope Ann 65
Melons 69
Not a Good Time for Six 73
A Painful Journey 77
The Dirty Dozen 81
A Wriggler and a Giggler 85
Miss Claire Brooks 89
Bad Times for Spanker Spage 93
Sniff Test 97
The Sacking of Spanker Spage 101

A Rambunctious Return

The first week that the inmates of the Woody Back to School unit returned to the facility following the Christmas furlough was a notoriously rambunctious time. The inmates had difficulty adjusting back to the strict regime of tutorials, lectures, supervised recreation and lock-downs.

The austere imposition of the zero-tolerance program code-named Operation Scorched Arse made the twelve inmates Ms Lawton had branded the 'Dirty Dozen' particularly vulnerable. The corridors were quickly filled with the sounds of canes, straps and slippers rebounding from tautened navy-blue gossamer bumbags.

It was a good time for Patty Hodge and her cohorts on the Radical Right and they went into action with religious zeal. Canings in the lecture rooms were at a premium as the Brass sought to reassert its power over the mischievous inmates.

It was good time for Yvonne Godfrey and her sycophantic disciples amongst the Secret Sorority of

A Year of Sitting Painfully

Serial Spankers. During the frenetic flurry of whops that greeted the New Year Yvonne had forgotten the vicious thrashing that Patty had given her at the end of the past term and was commanding her SS troops with renewed vigor.

Ms Lawton monitored the situation carefully. She read every punishment report thoroughly, looking for evidence that the Radical Right and SS were abusing their thrashing rights. Unfortunately for the inmates the Grand Dame was forced to concede that the lickings all appeared to be street legal and that every whop that the mega-minxes received was well-deserved.

Without interference from the Grand Dame Patty Hodge and Yvonne Godfrey considered themselves omnipotent.

From the perspective of bumbag preservation it was not a good time to be a mega-minx. Nonetheless, despite the proliferation of bumbag tattering the Dirty Dozen were undeterred and embarked on a campaign of renewed mischief and mayhem.

Predictably Jojo and her chums led the way. Joanna Heyworth was the undisputed queen of the Bottoms Up Table of Troublemakers, known colloquially to the inmates of the facility as the Big BUTT. During the first five days of her return to the facility Jojo was caned three times.

As usual Jojo took it in her stride and vowed to carry on minxing.

Deborah Morton's trials and tribulations continued. When she arrived for her first music tutorial of the term she hardly had time to sit down before Ms Whitton instructed her to fetch the Morton Special and step up before the form, accusing her of gross insolence.

Everybody in the room knew that the charge was bogus but there was little Debs could do but bend over the piano stool so that her arch-nemesis could beat her bandy with the customized violin bow.

Unbeknownst to Debs this was the start of an untoward trend that would continue for some time into the future.

Ms Lawton was suspicious over Ms Whitton's motives and quizzed the Dame of Musical Studies over the thrashing. Ms Whitton was extremely indignant at being questioned and fabricated a string of porkies to justify the beating. Ms Lawton was not entirely convinced. However, two days later Dotty Hammell, the darling of the Liberal Left, put Debs over her knee and spanked her with a wooden spoon. Ms Lawton concluded that Debs was up to her old tricks and shelved her investigation.

The other two members of the Famous Four, Nicola Jane Nixon and Rosemary Booker also both opened their new term whop accounts during the first week when they were sent up to the Grand Dame's study for six stroke bare benders.

Katie Beck was having a field day. The unit's matron had noticed that most of the inmates invested in new clobber during the furloughs and particularly new blouses which had taken the most wear and tear during the previous term.

A Year of Sitting Painfully

The inmates assumed that the new garments, straight out of their packaging, would be in pristine condition and rarely checked them thoroughly. To her delight Katie had found this expectation to be fatally flawed. During the first week of term she personally inspected every item of clobber handed in for laundry. She found many garments with factory flaws such as hanging threads or badly stitched seams. During the first week of term Katie slippered over a dozen startled inmates on charges of handing in their clobber in an abusive state.

As usual Penelope Ann Evans, the Red-shirt at the facility, vainly tried to curb the sadistic practices of Yvonne's heinous SS but Patty Hodge lambasted her and prohibited her from taking her concerns to the Grand Dame.

If the whop-rate during the opening week was any kind of gauge the inmates of the Woody Back to School unit predicted hot and sweaty times ahead of them.

Brats at Risk

One of the most critical roles amongst the Elite was the position of Senior Brat Draper. She had overall responsibility for monitoring the progress of the Brat mentoring program.

Penny Ann had been fiercely opposed to the proposal of Juliet Spage to fulfill the role. However, she was locked in a stalemate with Patty Hodge, the Deputy Grand Dame of the facility. Patty was determined to veto Cathryn Cassidy from being appointed in a senior role in the Elite organization. Pen was equally adamant that she would reject the nominations of Yvonne or Janet Mitchell. Patty proposed Juliet Spage as a compromise. Unfortunately for Penelope Ann with her other allies, Melanie White and the Butcher Twins, already appointed in key roles she did not have a suitable alternative candidate. She was forced to accede.

Penelope Ann had good reasons for opposing Juliet. The two gals had history. Several years earlier Pen had been mucking out the stables when she had

A Year of Sitting Painfully

smelled smoke. She had hurried to find the source and discovered a bale of hay burning in one of the stalls. Fortunately, there hadn't been any animals nearby and she was able to quell the fire without any harm apart from smoke damage.

There was an enquiry and a root cause analysis was performed. Several cigarette ends were found, along with two half-drunk cans of imported Jamaican brew. When Penny had been dashing to find the fire she had spotted Juliet Spage and Jayne Underly fleeing the scene.

Penny Ann had been interrogated and Ms Lawton accepted that she was an innocent party and that her quick response had saved the stables from more severe damage. However, the Grand Dame was convinced that Pen knew who the culprits were and wasn't saying. She proceeded to sweat Penny on a daily basis demanding her to give up the names. It was a disagreeable time for Penny Ann.

Finally Ms Lawton gave Pen an ultimatum, either give up the culprits or she would be publicly flogged for withholding evidence during Friday's Callover.

Penny even refused to tell her closest chums that Juliet and Jayne were responsible. Melanie and Cat counseled her that nobody would consider her a snitch under the circumstances but Penny Ann Evans stayed schtum.

On Friday evening Penny Ann appeared on stage dressed in whopping bags. Ms Lawton addressed the assembled inmates and demanded that the culprits come forward. When there was no response she gave Penny Ann a last opportunity to help her in her enquiries. Once again Pen refused and seemed resigned to bending over the vaulting horse to receive her first ever public flogging.

Ms Lawton was a pragmatist. There was little benefit in punishing an innocent party and it was clear that the true culprits were never going to come forward. She dismissed Penny from the stage with her whopping bags intact and filed her case notes under the category of 'Unsolved Mystery.'

Penelope Ann Evans and Juliet Spage had rarely spoken since the incident.

Katie Beck was particularly pleased by the appointment of Juliet Spage as Senior Brat Draper. She possessed many qualities that Katie considered made her a potentially all-time great Serial Spanker.

Juliet had already pledged her support to the SS and was a sycophantic disciple of Yvonne Godfrey. She was a notorious bully and most importantly she was extremely malleable.

"They'd better cover their arses, I'm coming in spanking," she assured Katie.

Katie expected great things of Juliet Spage.

It was not a good time to be a Little Brat. The Brats most at risk were those who had been allocated to grub for members of the SS. Disciplinary drapings and sporting spankings were at a premium. Grubby's were routinely turned over the knees of their Personal Drapers to have their bumbags dusted.

If that wasn't bad enough Juliet Spage established a slew of new performance criteria that she insisted the Little Brats complied with. Each evening she would summons one of the Brat Pack to

A Year of Sitting Painfully

her study and chide them for poor performance before putting them over her knee.

She boasted to her chums over her daily bumbag dustings. She introduced a new recreation for the SS. Often she would summons some unfortunate grubby to her own study and have her toast crumpets in the fireplace. While the grubby was bent over Juliet and her SS friends would gleefully fire pellets at the grubby's arse with high-powered catapults. The SS considered this pastime rib tickling fun.

The unfortunate Brats were not so amused and began to refer to her as Spanker Spage.

A Grubby Life

Brat Rights had never been a high priority. Ms Lawton knew that every year twelve of the nations most Extreme Ladettes would be handed into her custody to embark on their programs of Extreme Social Rehabilitation.

These young women were generally infamous for their wild partying and boisterous behavior. The Grand Dame knew that it was imperative that they were immediately inducted into the rules, regulations and protocols and cured of any truculent or rebellious tendencies.

She could think of no better way to bring the new inmates into line than to have them act as grubby's and to spend some quality mentoring time head down, arse up across the laps of the Brass and the Elite.

The practice of grubbing was steeped in history. It was originally a term used in Edwardian private boarding schools where miscreant gals were

A Year of Sitting Painfully

sent out to grub around in the gardens as punishment for misbehavior.

When the pioneering suffragettes, the Lawrence Sisters, founded the original Woody School in 1857 they offered the new entrants a full academic curriculum which had only previously been available to the young male population.

They fashioned their school on the strict academic and disciplinary principles of Eton and Winchester, including introducing the grubbing program that was a variation of the tradition of 'fagging' that had originated at the two schools during the 16th Century.

Woodys was a huge success and was populated by the daughters of the nation's nobility, landed gentry, intellectuals and influential politicians.

In a memoir authored by the Duchess of Meddlethorpe, one of the first females to sit in parliament she laments, "During my first months as a Woody gal I was draped across the knees of my Grub-mistress as often as three times a week to be spanked for failing to grub up to the expected standards." However, she also admits that her time as a grubby set her in good stead to face up to the challenges of life ahead of her.

During her first year as a boarder at the original Woody School Ms Lawton had been entered into the Brat Mentoring program and assigned a Personal Draper.

Between cleaning, scrubbing and running endless errands she took frequent trips across her Draper's knee to be spanked for any shortcomings, perceived or otherwise.

Although the practice of grubbing had largely been phased out in the conventional education system Ms Lawton elected to resurrect the practice when the Woody Back to School unit had opened its doors a decade earlier.

Even Penelope Ann's liberal allies paid little heed to the plight of the Little Brats. They had all been subjected to the same program and reasoned that the Brats should consider themselves lucky to be getting off with hand-spankings instead of having the cane taken to their arses. Brat Rights were low on their agenda.

Spanker Spage religiously reported the details of her daily dustings to Katie Beck. Katie would stretch the rules and pour Spanker a glass of wine while she enjoyed spank-by-spank accounts of Juliet's latest successes.

The unit matron encouraged Juliet to be more adventurous. Over the past few years, she explained, the Brat Protocols had changed. Ever since Ms Lawton had established the precedent of caning Joanna Heyworth during her Bratyear several other ne'er-do-wells had been inducted into the Beaten Brat Club.

Katie suggested that Spanker could use the threat of filing applications for certain Brats to be beaten for serial malfeasance to her advantage. Katie offered Spanker the loan of several of her collection of leather-soled slippers.

"They will much prefer a slippering than a visit to the Beak for the cane," Katie assured Spanker, pouring her another glass of wine. "Just be prudent, dear Spanker, be very, very prudent."

A Year of Sitting Painfully

At first Spanker followed Katie's advise. She limited her illicit slippering activity to the unfortunate backsides of the personal grubby's of her cronies amongst the SS.

Under the threat of being caned by Ms Lawton her victims dismally acceded to repairing to hidden areas of the vast compound to have their rumps pummeled with the unforgiving slippers.

As Spanker's illicit dustings continued without comment or reprimand her confidence grew and she became increasingly cocksure.

It was not a good time to be a grubby.

Even Brats Have Rights

Jennifer Gardiner was draped face downwards across Spanker Spage's lap with her skirt turned back and her bumbags concertinaed around her ankles. Spanker was applying the leather sole of one of Katie's slippers to Jennifer's backside with extreme vigor.

"What the dickens?" asked Ms Lummell in amazement. "What the devil do you think you're up to Spage? Release her immediately!"

Juliet Spage stared aghast at the Riding Dame. This was not supposed to have happened. She had carefully planned the slippering to coincide with a staff meeting scheduled by Ms Lawton and a riding party to be out on the Downs. The stables were supposed to empty. She gaped at Ms Lummell.

"I said release her!" snapped the Dame tartly.

Slowly Juliet turned down Jennifer's skirt and helped her to her feet. Jen crouched down and retrieved her bumbags and slipped them back into place. She threw a hostile glance at Spanker.

A Year of Sitting Painfully

Jane Lummell wasted no time; she barreled down on Spanker and yanked her to her feet. She span the prefect around and took a tight grip on the scruff of her neck.

"Come with me!" she said authoritatively.

Juliet could do nothing but splutter and comply as she was hustled out of the stables under a full collar.

The quadrangle and recreation areas were bustling with activity but everybody stopped as the inmates witnessed the unusual sight of a member of the Elite being subjected to a collaring.

Juliet was an immensely unpopular member of the community and was one of the most active practitioners of the fine art of collaring. There was little sympathy for her plight.

"This is Elite business, Jane," said Patty Hodge smoothly. "I'll take care of Miss Spage myself."

"I brought her here first out of courtesy," said Jane Lummell firmly. "She's going up before the Beak. Even Brats have rights, whether you like it or not. I'm giving you the opportunity to accompany us, Patricia, but I really couldn't care less one way or the other."

Patty scowled. "There is no need to be hasty, I'm sure that there is a perfectly good explanation, why don't we let Miss Spage give us her version of events?"

Jane Lummell shook her head. "She's coming with me," she said spinning Juliet around and shoving her towards the door. "Are you coming, Patricia?"

Jane Lummell was a good old-fashioned jolly hockey sticks kind of cove. She served in the dual role of Dame in Charge of Physical Education and Riding. She fulfilled both roles with enthusiasm and dedication and was well-liked by the inmates. She generously gave up considerable amounts of her free-time with Deborah Morton and Rachel Cox to keep them in shape to eventually resume their tennis careers. She also helped numerous other celebrity athletes that had fallen foul of the Systems anti-Ladetting laws.

Jane was a fully paid up member of the Liberal Left of the Brass and was tight with Dotty Hammell, Stephanie Powell and Pauline Gascoigne. She was considered generally minx-friendly, nonetheless she was a strict disciplinarian and was lethal with both her over-sized rubber-soled plimsoll and her braided riding crop. She was considered reliable by the inmates and when she instructed them to bend over for whops there was rarely much doubt that they were well-deserved.

Juliet Spage was not holding up well under interrogation. Patty did her best to intercede, claiming that protocols had been broken and that she had the first right of interview. It was not that she cared two figs about the fate of Spanker Spage; she just didn't want the Grand Dame poking around in Radical Right business.

Ms Lawton fixed Patty with a withering glare. "This is bullying business, Patricia," she said sharply, "and that is my business."

A Year of Sitting Painfully

Patty just shrugged. "You're quite right, Susan," she said unctuously and turned on Juliet. "Well Spage, aren't you going to explain yourself?" she snapped spitefully. "The cat got your tongue?"

Dolefully, Spanker Spage stared down at the floor.

At first the prefect had claimed that the slippering was an isolated incident and she apologized profusely, even agreeing that a flogging was appropriate. However, further probing soon exposed the scale of the brutality she had inflicted upon the helpless Little Brats.

A Flogging for Spanker Spage

"Hand over your tie, blazer, badges and your ashplant," the Grand Dame informed Juliet Spage in front of the assembled inmates. "You are formally stood down from the Elite."

Juliet hung her head in shame. Tears rolled down her cheeks as she shrugged off her blazer and handed it Penelope Ann Evans. She loosened her tie and unknotted it and handed that over too.

"My ashplant's in my study," she muttered.

"It will no longer be your study, Spage," Ms Lawton informed her coldly. "For the remainder of your sentence you will reside in the Brat Dorm and be returned to the Brat program. You will wear full clobber and I shall arrange for you to be scheduled in for grubbing duties. Although you will continue your educational curriculum as normal, to all extents and purposes you are now a Little Brat."

Juliet continued to sob.

Ms Lawton looked over her classes. "You are in the final year of your Social Rehabilitation Program and you now have only six months left to prove to me

A Year of Sitting Painfully

that you have reformed. I shall be watching you carefully and I'm putting you on notice that if I see any signs of repetition of your bullying tendencies I will formally flunk you and send you before a Special Disciplinary hearing of the System. Now bend over the horse. I intend to flog you soundly."

The poor beleaguered Little Brats watched with satisfaction as Spanker Spage folded her frame over the vaulting horse. She had not gone quietly, she had wept and pleaded that she was not responsible. She blamed Patty and Katie and Yvonne for instructing her to perform the illicit slipperings. Ms Lawton curtly cut her short and instructed her to bend over the horse.

"I will have you held down if necessary," she promised Spanker.

Spanker made a muff of herself. She squealed and screamed and kicked up such a brouhaha that the watching inmates had to hide their mouths with their hands to keep from giggling.

There was no question that public floggings were tough duty. Being folded in half across a vaulting horse with the full compliment of the inmates and Brass staring at her upturned arse was no fun for a gal. Nonetheless, ever since April Turner had taken the first ever public flogging in stoic silence the Woody gals had prided themselves in the manner with which they conducted themselves when obliged to grace the stage.

Ms Lawton sighed. The manner with which Juliet Spage was conducting herself was beginning to give her the pip.

"Good grief, Spage," she barked. "Cease those ridiculous noises or I'll really give you something to howl about."

The inmates chuckled at that.

Spanker Spage was making a muff of herself. She was dancing an idiot gig and rubbing her backside frantically.

"Stand still, you foolish gal," snapped Ms Lawton, "I have never seen such a pathetic performance. Now stand still this instant before I cane you again."

Juliet Spage looked haggard and bereft of dignity, standing on the stage with her white tieless blouse buttoned to the throat and white whopping bags. The small amount of make-up she was allowed to wear was smudged and her hair looked lank and unkempt. Her eyes were red-rimmed and her nose was dripping.

Patty Hodge gaped at the Grand Dame. She gnashed her teeth and wrung her hands in consternation. Ms Lawton had just announced that Cathryn Cassidy would replace Juliet in the role of Senior Brat Draper. To Patty it was an unforgivable act of betrayal by Ms Lawton. She had made the decision unilaterally without consultation with her deputy. Patty hurried from the stage and headed for the saloon bar of the Bunch of Grapes.

A Year of Sitting Painfully

Katie gaped at Ms Lawton. "She's telling you a pack of porkies," she insisted. "I most certainly did not lend her one of my slippers; she must have snuck into my office and stolen it."

Ms Lawton rolled her eyes. She had little doubt that her adopted daughter was being economical with the truth but she had no hard evidence that Katie had acted as Spanker's sponsor.

"Be careful, Katie," she told her ward. "I'm watching you."

Ms Lawton's Exit Strategy

Juliet Spage gloomily pulled on the temporary gymslip that Katie had supplied. Katie had purposefully selected one that was undersized and Spanker had difficulty fastening the buttons at the shoulders. The garment was so short that it barely covered her bumbags.

Cat Cassidy was sitting with her long legs swinging loosely over the arm of an easy chair. She was flexing her ashplant between her hands.

"Hurry along Spage," she said sharply, "we haven't got all night and I've got plenty of errands for you to run before lock-down."

Spanker was still teary-eyed. Her backside was throbbing incessantly. The news that she was being allocated to grub for Cathryn had sounded like the death knell.

Despite Cat's laid-back demeanor she scared the crap out of Juliet. On several occasions Cathryn had tackled Spanker regarding her predilection for delivering sporting spankings. Cat had warned the

A Year of Sitting Painfully

Senior Brat Draper to keep her hands off her personal grubby and Spanker had wisely complied.

She hurriedly knotted her tie and tucked it into the bib of her gymslip.

"What would you like me to start with?" she asked and quickly added, "Ma'am," when Cat raised an eyebrow.

"It's an absolute abomination," Patty was whining in the saloon bar of the Bunch of Grapes. "Cassidy is a subversive; she'll poke her nose into SS business now that she has a senior position."

Katie and the Wart nodded dutifully. They were well aware of Patty's obsessive hatred of Cat Cassidy and they settled in for a long night of her bitching and moaning.

Ms Lawton poured herself a glass of chilled 2004 Altosour Sauvignon Blanc and kicked back in an easy chair. She was feeling quite satisfied with the days proceedings. She smiled to herself at the thought of Patty Hodge kvetching in the saloon bar of the Bunch of Grapes and sipped her drink.

During the Christmas furlough Ms Lawton had spent several hours wining and dining with the Minister of Extreme Social Rehabilitation. He had been disappointed when she had tendered her resignation with effect at the end of the present year. Nonetheless, she had been adamant that she had achieved all she could and that it was time for a change.

"I assume Ms Hodge will take over?" asked the Minister.

Ms Lawton chose her words carefully. "Patricia is a brilliant academic and has designed some of our finest learning programs," she told the Minister. "She has supported me over the past ten years, for which I am indebted. However, I feel that her thinking is too entrenched. I honestly believe that we need to look for a candidate from outside the Unit."

"That won't be easy," said the Minister. "A decade ago when we began recruiting there was a large pool of experienced disciplinarians available to us. These days with the liberals and all their STOPP nonsense we'd be hard pressed to find a Grand Dame who even knows how to use a cane these days."

"Then look outside the education system," suggested Ms Lawton. "That's how you found me."

The Minister smiled and patted Ms Lawton's hand. "You are somewhat unique, Susan," he told her. "But, I'll scout the market and get back to you. If I can't locate a candidate I suppose we'll use Ms Hodge as our fall-back position?"

"No, Minister" said Ms Lawton emphatically. "Anybody except Patricia."

Ms Lawton stared down at the piece of paper. To say the details were scant was an understatement. The resume merely identified a man named Mr Humphries, cited his career history as classified, and a security ranking that gave him direct access to the Prime Minister and the cabinet.

"This is not much to go on," said Ms Lawton.

The Minister shrugged. "I'm sorry but that is all we're going to get. However, you can interview him personally when he returns from the Baltic's in a few weeks. I think you'll like him. He comes highly recommended."

"Hmmm," said Ms Lawton. "At least you're making this intriguing."

Ms Lawton poured a second glass of wine. Tomorrow morning she would drive up to the Smoke to meet the man named Humphries in person. It was an intriguing proposition, and of course one that would send poor Patty into a fit of apoplexy if she found out. Ms Lawton knew that she would have to execute her exit strategy in total secrecy.

Hurricane Jojo

Joanna Heyworth lowered herself gingerly onto the unforgiving seat of the wooden chair. At the front of the lecture room Ms Powell was hanging her cane back on the hook beside the blackboard.

Jojo wriggled forward slightly so that her weight was supported by the backs of her thighs and the direct pressure was relieved from her sizzling buttocks.

Ms Powell turned back and continued with her lecture on the comparative merits of Mailer and Roth. Stephanie Powell was considered to be a very good thing by the inmates. She was a first class instructor and was unquestionably inclined towards the liberal left of the Brass. Nonetheless, when duty called she was a dab hand with the whippy number one cane.

Jojo had awoken in a mischievous mood despite the fact that she was sporting a sore arse. The previous evening she and her best chum, Nixdown, had been forced to bend over the ends of

A Year of Sitting Painfully

their beds for six hot ones from Melanie White for gabbing after lock-down.

The late-night licking had been another landmark Jojo punishment. She had broken her own record for being the fastest inmate to accumulate twenty-five canings during a single year.

Over brekker her fellow mega-minxes were quick to congratulate her. Since the launch of Operation Scorched Arse competition on the Hall of Shame had intensified. Faced with a policy of zero-tolerance the inmates had thrown caution to the wind and bumbag tattering was at a record high. Jojo's new record was something to be celebrated and respected.

Jojo celebrated her new record by acquiring yellow cards during each of the first three lectures of the day. She japed and larked, goofed and pranked and wound the Brass up a treat. Her chums watched her with amused resignation. She was in classic Hurricane Jojo form and they knew from experience that there was nothing that they could do to deter her.

Joanna Heyworth's rise to the pinnacle of the Hall of Shame had been the result of relentless minxing. Now in the fifth year of her sentence she had over-taken legendary über-minxes such as April Turner, Cat Cassidy, Lady Victoria Brompton and Claire Brooks to become the undisputed Big BUTT.

Ms Powell narrowed her eyes. The Dame in charge of English Studies was nobody's fool. She was fond of Jojo. Despite the inmate's errant tendencies she was brilliant, articulate and vivacious. Nonetheless, Stephanie Powell knew when she was being played like a fish. She reached into her jacket pocket and extracted her yellow card.

"Alright, enough already, Heyworth," she snapped. "One more peep out of you and you'll be bending over your desk."

"Yes, Ma'am," said Jojo contritely. "Sorry, Ma'am."

Jojo slid her vintage Renwal Roto Blaster out of her satchel and palmed it. She glanced about the lecture room. Ms Powell had her back turned, writing up their assignment on the blackboard, her fellow students were bent over their books taking notes. She contemplated her options.

Nicola Jane Nixon was still grumpy over the six they had received the previous night. Rosemary Booker was slightly out of range. Debs Morton was seated slightly in front of her and a perfect target. Jojo turned the nozzle to the spray setting, raised her pistol and took aim.

"Whoa, what the fuck?" exclaimed Deborah. Debs had been leaning over her text-book taking notes when her concentration was rudely interrupted. She span around angrily, water dripping from her hair.

Ms Powell also span around, taking in the situation. Debs was glaring around the room, squeezing her hair as water dripped onto the shoulder of her blazer. The other inmates were all looking sublimely innocent.

A Year of Sitting Painfully

"I shall pretend I didn't hear that, Morton," said Ms Powell quite calmly. "Now will whoever is responsible for this disruption please fess up or do I have to instigate a needless inquisition?"

With a cheerful smile on her face Jojo slid her water pistol across the lid of her desk.

Never a Truer Word Spoken in Jest

Deborah frowned at Jojo. "You could have got me whopped," she complained.

Joanna hugged her chum. "Sorry about that," she said consolingly. "But you know that all's fair in love and minxing. I just had an overwhelming moment."

"Grrrrrrrrr!' grumbled Deborah Morton. "And you knew I've still got a slight touch of the residuals."

Jojo grinned. "Oh yes, I forgot you got whopped yesterday," she said half-apologetically. "Sorry about that."

Deborah Morton stared bleakly at the Economics Dame.

"Remove your blazer and bend over the desk," Ms Gascoigne had instructed her. "I intend to absolutely cream you."

The Woody gals were used to Pauline Gascoigne's colorful expressions but this was a new one. Debs wasn't sure what being absolutely creamed

A Year of Sitting Painfully

entailed but she had the distinct feeling that it was not going to be pleasant.

There was no question that Deborah needed six of the best. She had been caught with a proverbial smoking gun, or at least a high powered catapult loaded with a paper pellet and cocked ready to fire.

Of course Deborah couldn't allow her dousing from Jojo to go unreciprocated, no self-respecting minx would have. Nonetheless, her timing had sucked. Not in the least due to the fact that just twenty-four hours earlier she had bent over her desk for a very sound six from the same Dame who was now announcing her intention to absolutely cream her.

Pauline and Deborah had a long history. They had schooled together at the Queensgate Academy and had been tight. They had a good deal in common. Both were academically brilliant and Pauline was one of the few tennis players with the capability of occasionally taking a game or two from Debs. They were also acknowledged as being two of the naughtiest girls in the school.

However, when Deborah was in the fourth form the dynamic of their relationship altered dramatically. Pauline was extremely popular and had been unanimously voted in to take up the position of President of Posh, the school's prefectorial body. Deborah had voted for her and helped with her campaign.

It was a mercurial year for Deborah. She deposed Rachel Cox as the nation's number one tennis player, was selected to play the clarinet in the National Youth Orchestra and published a widely acclaimed fictional biography of Mary Queen of Scots titled 'Waiting to be Beheaded'. She also established a school record for being 'Put on the Menu' and having to appear before disciplinary hearings hosted by the Posh.

It was a tribute to Deborah's articulate advocacy that she was 'Put on the Menu' over one hundred times during the school year but was only sentenced to be beaten on nine occasions.

Despite their friendship Deborah never expected special treatment from the President. Pauline had a reputation for being lethal with the ceremonial popping stick and she caned Deborah just as hard as she would anybody else.

During the last week of the school year Deborah had excelled herself by being 'Put on the Menu' three times in a single day. All the charges she faced had been entered in the first degree.

Audaciously Deborah elected to plead not guilty to all three charges. Although she managed to successfully defend herself against one of the charges the odds were stacked against her. The Posh found her guilty of serial misconduct and she was sentenced to receive the maximum punishment of nine strokes of the popping stick for both of the remaining offenses. She would receive nine strokes immediately and then be allowed a twenty-four hour cool down period before returning for the second thrashing. Pauline Gascoigne had looked genuinely sympathetic when she delivered the bad news.

Despite everything they remained fast friends and on the eve of Deborah's infamous Wimbledon

A Year of Sitting Painfully

semi-final they dined together, along with Christy Cranfield, another former President of Posh.

Pauline had news for her chums. After completing her degree she had been investigating the job market. She had been considering several opportunities when she was head-hunted by Ms Lawton.

Pauline Gascoigne possessed all the characteristics the Grand Dame was seeking. She was academically brilliant and had shown her mettle as the President of Posh, when she had delivered over three hundred and fifty canings. Ms Lawton opened her cheque book.

At the time Deborah had already been charged under the anti-Ladette laws. Her agents had brokered a deal with the System that she would serve a minimum sentence at the Radcliffe Back to School unit. She would be allowed to play in the minimum amount of professional tournaments to maintain her Grand Prix status.

As the three chums left the restaurant in plenty of time for Deborah to keep to the curfew imposed by the Dark Agents Pauline had hugged Debs.

"Now go straight home," she giggled, "else I'll find myself back bending you over for six."

The three friends had laughed, but never has a truer word been said in jest. Within twenty-four hours Deborah Morton was arrested on live television and sentenced to seven years at the Big House without the possibility of parole.

Absolutely Creamed

Deborah slithered her chest across the desktop and reached down and gripped the legs on the far side. She heard Ms Gascoigne approaching and waited to be caned.

Pauline Gascoigne tapped the legs of the desk with the tip of her cane. "Reach down further," she told Debs.

Deborah stretched over a little.

"Further," Pauline instructed her.

Debs pushed her legs up and slithered even further forward. She was bent so far over the desk that if she went forward any further she was in danger of tumbling down and landing on her head. Deborah Morton was acutely aware that her backside was stuck up in the air in the most prominent position physically possible. She felt as if her backside might shortly eclipse the sun. She was beginning to sweat.

Pauline Gascoigne neatly turned back the hem of Deborah's navy blue pleated skirt and then retrieved her cane. She stepped to one side and

A Year of Sitting Painfully

unhurriedly began her preparations, taking her measure and tapping the cane down once, twice and then thrice. She raised her arm and sliced the whippy rattan stick through the air, landing it crisply across the sweet spot of Debs' bottom with an explosive crack. Even Deborah's whop-hardened inmates were impressed.

Deborah Morton was in little position for refined analysis. Her backside was a well-calibrated whopometer and the first strike was enough to confirm that being absolutely creamed was not going to be much fun. The heat of the cane lashing across her backside ricocheted around her central nervous system like a pinball.

Pauline Gascoigne was widely popular amongst the inmates. She was considered even-handed and minx-friendly. Nonetheless, she was highly respected around the community as a consummate artiste with a cane. She hardly seemed to be trying but there was little doubt in anybody's mind that she was giving Deborah a power-whopping.

Pauline Gascoigne prided herself that she could administer discipline dispassionately. During her period as the President of Posh at the Queensgate Academy she rarely had to use her casting vote. Most cases were open and closed and when required she was merely responsible for delivering the punishment as safely as possible. Nonetheless, she was quite irritated by Deborah's ridiculous performance.

Deborah Morton was beginning to deeply regret her ill-fated attempt at revenge. The cane was colliding with her bumbags with alarming ferocity. She was feeling quite giddy.

Pauline Gascoigne took her time. Despite her initial irritation at Deborah's guileless prank she had taken several deep breaths and regained her composure.

The previous day she had caned Debs on routine business after she had continued to goof after several verbal warnings and a yellow card. Pauline had delivered a good crisp six that she had expected would give the errant inmate something to think about for a few days. Clearly the six had not been quite stiff enough so she felt obliged to step up the pace. She raised her arm and brought the cane down with a mighty crack.

Debs hung over the desk panting. Five strokes in and just one left to go. Her backside was already throbbing incessantly. She braced herself for what she suspected was going to be a very grand finale. She heard a whistle from behind her and then her whole body wriggled and writhed in distress as the long thin cane rebounded from her bumbags with nerve-jangling, teeth-chattering force.

Deborah handed over her punishment record book with trembling fingers. Her cheeks were ashen and she had a slightly bemused look on her face.

Debs was no newcomer to being soundly thrashed. She had an unfortunate tendency of bringing out the worst in the Brass and the Elite.

A Year of Sitting Painfully

Nonetheless, she couldn't help thinking that her most recent excursion across her desk had been something rather special.

Barely able to keep from hopping up and down on the spot, Deborah Morton now fully comprehended what it meant to be absolutely creamed.

Miss Lisa Sutton

Despite their discomfort Jojo and Debs had cause for celebration. In the competitive world of the Hall of Shame the two Phase 5 inmates knew that every whop counted. Although Jojo was the undisputed Big BUTT Deborah was always just behind her, snapping at her bumbags. Once the two chums' backsides had begun to cool down they both agreed it had been a good day's work.

Lisa Sutton stood outside the library with her hands on her head and her nose pressed to the wall. Along the corridor she could hear the approaching footsteps of Yvonne Godfrey and Janet Mitchell. She felt an uncomfortable knot in her tummy.
Unlike Jojo, Debs and the other dedicated über-minxes, Lisa Sutton had no aspirations for making headlines on the Hall of Shame.
Lisa had originally been sentenced to two years at the less austere Radcliffe Back to School unit on charges of Misdemeanor Ladetting. It was not hard time and she had occupied herself completing her

A Year of Sitting Painfully

studies in advanced physics. She was a popular member of the Radcliffe community and was well-known for her generosity in helping other inmates with their academic endeavors.

However, towards the end of her sentence at the facility she found herself falsely accused of writing papers for other inmates to support their applications for further education. Lisa denied the charges vehemently.

Unlike the Big House, as Woodys was known amongst the Ladette community, the Radcliffe Back to School unit did not practice corporal punishment. However, despite her denials the Principal of the facility took the unprecedented action of procuring a cane and giving Lisa three strokes across the palm of her left hand.

Lisa was outraged and filed a complaint with her Court Appointed Guardian. Several days later she was summonsed before a special hearing of the System where she fully expected to be exonerated. Instead she listened incredulously while she was found guilty of 'Subversion of the Back to School system, making false statements and accepting bribes to pervert the university application system.' She was sentenced to a further five years of Extreme Social Rehabilitation to be served at the Big House.

Before arriving at the facility she spent a week of immersion induction into the rules, regulations and protocols that would dominate her short-term future.

Upon arriving at the unit it only took two days for Lisa to learn the harsh realities of her new life. She was forced to bend over her bed to be given six strokes by the Dorm Raider for gabbing after lock-down.

The punishment caused her to memorably observe that, "three strokes of the cane across your left hand hardly prepares you for six hot ones across the seat of thin pajamas!"

Despite the austere environment she found herself in, Lisa Sutton settled in quickly. She was particularly impressed by the comprehensive academic curriculum Ms Lawton had established and the quality of the tutoring provided by the Dames. It was immediately clear that she was an academic phenomenon, particularly in the areas of maths and science and Ms Lawton arranged for her to continue her studies in advanced physics under the guidance of Ms MacAllister.

Lisa's fellow inmates did their best to make her feel at home, but they had already spent two years incarcerated together and had formed bonds and friendships that Lisa found hard to penetrate.

During her first term at the facility Lisa was caned twice more. Not for anything serious, just routine goofing, gabbing, larking and pranking. She impressed her fellow inmates by embracing the Woody creed that only muffs howl and took her lickings with admirable stoicism.

She studied Cathryn Cassidy's 'Manifesto of Mega-minxdom', but was not an instant convert. Whilst she could appreciate the joys of minxing she was considerably averse to rattan rebounding off her bumbags. She became skilled at limiting her misbehavior to the extent of attracting yellow cards and avoiding unnecessary canings. Lisa gained the reputation for being naughty but nice.

A Year of Sitting Painfully

Although Lisa's peers continued to warm to her she still considered herself an outsider. Due to the proximity of the surnames in the alphabet Lisa Sutton found herself seated next to Bernadette Summers during lectures and tutorials, and in the bed beside her in the dorm. She couldn't help observing that Bernadette was something of an outsider herself.

Miss Bernadette Summers

Lisa Sutton remembered Bernadette from her notorious court appearances over a decade earlier. Bernadette Summers was the daughter of shamed and incarcerated Sri-Lankan diplomat, Joe Summers. During her father's trial the defense had done their best to exploit his teenage daughter, dressing Bernadette in a gymslip, blouse and tie, scrubbing her face clean of make-up and tying her hair back in pig-tails.

She had adamantly defended her father as a misunderstood and philanthropic man. She withstood two days of intense and increasingly hostile cross-examination by the prosecution giving a wonderfully crafted display of girlish charm and naivety. She steadfastly refused to acknowledge the whereabouts of the millions of quids that the nefarious diplomat had squirreled into offshore bank accounts.

Nobody was fooled. In his summation the judge described Bernadette as precociously conniving and accused her of effortlessly perjuring herself

A Year of Sitting Painfully

throughout the trial. He condemned her as a willing participant in her father's confidence trickery.

Joe Summers was sentenced to fifteen years in chokey and Bernadette was sent to reform school.

Once she was released Bernadette joined the growing ranks of the Ladettes. She quickly accumulated several charges of Extreme Ladetting and thought it best to have it on her toes to the South of France. She prospered as a professional gambler and was sublimely unaware that the Dark Agents of the System had targeted her as a prime candidate for a stretch in the Big House.

They enticed her home with bogus claims that her father was in poor health. Bernadette flew home straight into seven years of Whops and Clobber.

Outwardly Bernadette was a surly cove. Her peripatetic youth bouncing from country to country, always just one step ahead of Plod had made her secretive and self-reliant. At Woodys she had wasted no time in establishing Bernadette Summers Enterprises which specialized in providing the incarcerated Ladettes with access to booze, fags and other contraband.

Lisa had attempted to engage Bernadette in conversation but was generally met with polite but guarded platitudes. Once when she tried to offer Bernadette sympathy after a whopping the dusky beauty told her, "I was caned in Cairo, slippered in Singapore and whacked in Washington. They can't hurt me, I'm the fucking Bounder!"

As Lisa's first Christmas approached she noticed that Bernadette was even more sullen than usual. Nervously Lisa approached the Bounder and asked what was wrong. Surprisingly Bernadette didn't bite her face off but, instead, confided that she hated furloughs.

With her old chap banged up in chokey, she explained, the System had appointed her brother as her custodial ward. Her brother, who she described as a waste of valuable spunk, was intent on learning the whereabouts of Joe Summers ill-gotten gains. Bernadette was equally intent in keeping them secret.

"When Pop get's out," she told Lisa. "We're going to be swapping canes for Cannes and that little scumbag ain't gonna see a penny."

She told Lisa that in attempt to break her spirit her brother allowed his girlfriend to regularly put Bernadette over her knee and spank her with a slipper. The fact that her brother's girlfriend was several years younger than Bernadette did not help the situation.

Generously Lisa offered to put Bernadette up at her family pile over Christmas. "Pa's never there," she told the Bounder, "he's sailing one of his yachts around the Caribbean. Ma won't mind, she's certifiably barking and spends most of her time in her room. We'll have the run of the place."

During the furlough Bernadette slowly revealed the full extent of her enterprises back at the facility. What surprised Lisa was that the Bounder didn't seem to know whether the venture was profitable. Apparently money came in and money went out and as long as Bernadette's blazer pockets were crammed full of quids that was all she cared about. Lisa patiently explained the basic principles of cash-flow economics and offered to help her arrange her affairs, in return for seven and a half per cent, of course. Bernadette immediately agreed.

It was during that Christmas furlough that the two entrepreneurs decided to expand Bernadette's gambling arm of the enterprise. Historically the inmates had been able to place bets with the Bounder on the dogs and the nags. At Lisa's suggestion, they agreed to establish the 'Big BUTT Stakes', where the inmates would be able to wager on the outcome of the Hall of Shame.

It would prove to be Bernadette Summers Enterprise's most lucrative endeavor.

Bogus Whops

Janet Mitchell stepped up behind Lisa and spitefully twisted her ear.

"Get your arse inside," she growled. "I'll teach you to rubbish me, you little bitch. You ain't got Summers here to protect you now."

Lisa flinched at the pain in her ear and lowered her arms from above her head. Janet roughly turned her around and pushed her towards the door. Yvonne grinned wolfishly as she turned the handle.

Lisa trudged into the library and set off towards the fireplace. Behind her Yvonne and Mitch the Bitch were carrying on a disparaging commentary. Lisa did her best to ignore them.

Janet Mitchell's claim that Lisa had rubbished her was a stretch at best. She had been crossing the quadrangle minding her own business when she had been accosted by the two prefects.

"What's the time?" they had demanded.

Lisa had shrugged and shown them her left wrist. "I ain't wearing my watch," she said, "but let's see now." She pointed towards the unit's chapel.

A Year of Sitting Painfully

"Well the big hands nearly halfway around and the smaller hand's approaching six so that would make it what?"

Janet scowled. "I'll tell you who's approaching six," she snarled. "You are. Now get your arse up to the library."

Lisa glared at Mitch the Bitch. "Don't be ridiculous. You can see perfectly well what time it is. You ain't whopping me for this."

Janet turned to Yvonne. "You hear that Godders?" she asked. "She says she ain't going to be whopped. She blatantly rubbishes me in front of a witness and now she's refusing to report to the library."

Yvonne shook her head in disbelief. "I heard her. It's an outrage Bitchypoo, but if she won't go we can't make her. I guess we'll just have to file an application with Ms Hodge to have her publicly flogged," said the prefect.

"I'm sure that Ms Lawton would love that," grinned Janet. "What do you think, Sutters, old gal?"

Momentarily Lisa's stomach churned and she felt quite bilious. She knew that she was being stitched up like a kipper.

"This is so fucking bogus," she muttered and turned on her heel and headed towards the cloisters.

"Where do you think you're going?" demanded Janet.

"To the library," replied Lisa through clenched teeth.

Yvonne and Janet Mitchell winked at each other.

Lisa Sutton was bent forward at the waist with her fingers balanced on the tips of her toes. Her calf and thigh muscles stretched uncomfortably while Yvonne and Janet stood behind her swishing their ashplants playfully through the air.

Despite her indignation at being subjected to bogus whops it was a far preferable option than a trip up before the Grand Dame.

Lisa Sutton was a perfect target for the evil bullies of the SS. Spotting her crossing the quadrangle without the protection of the Bounder had been an ideal opportunity for Yvonne and Janet to have some fun. They both knew that all they had to do was trump up some charges and then threaten to involve Ms Lawton and Lisa would be forced to accede to a whopping.

For the majority of the first year of her incarceration at the Woody facility Lisa had maintained a relatively low profile. She had immersed herself in two projects, researching for a thesis she planned to write and expanding the profit base of Bernadette Summers Enterprises.

She was caned occasionally, generally for low-level minxing. Lisa was a cheerful, good-humored sort and took her licks without complaint. She was a popular and well-liked member of the community.

One Saturday in the spring, Lisa had been granted a town pass and had spent a pleasant afternoon at an art gallery. She had become so engrossed in studying the collection of a local photographer that she had forgotten the time. She

A Year of Sitting Painfully

had raced back to the facility but when she arrived the gates were locked. If she rang the bell it would mean that she would soon be cutting along for six of the best from the Duty Dame. Fortunately there was nobody in sight so she surreptitiously made her way around the walls of the grounds until she found an appropriately positioned tree. She clambered up and peeked over the wall. When she was sure that the coast was clear, she shimmied over the wall and hastily headed for the safety of the main building. Lisa was feeling quite smug when she arrived in the common room. Not only had she avoided an unpleasant six but she was back just in time for Callover and nobody would be any the wiser.

Low Riders

Lisa's smugness was short lived. Suddenly the doors of the common room burst open and the Grand Dame stormed in. She barreled down on the startled Lisa, yanked her out of her seat, span her around, pushing her down over the arm of the chair and yanking back her skirt.

Lisa's chum's watched in amazement. They had never seen Ms Lawton in such a tizzy and for her to make an impromptu appearance in the common-room was unprecedented.

There was no question that the Grand Dame was somewhat vexed. She slashed the senior cane downwards with extraordinary venom. The common-room echoed with six sharp cracks of the cane and then the Grand Dame yanked Lisa back to her feet and hustled her from the room. Lisa's chum's exchanged bewildered glances.

It transpired that Lisa's inopportune landing spot had been Ms Lawton's personal garden and in her haste she had plowed across several flowerbeds

A Year of Sitting Painfully

and caused considerable damage to the Grand Dame's seedlings. As fate would have it Ms Lawton had been at the window of her quarters when Lisa made her untimely break for freedom.

Lisa could not have made a more catastrophic error. The Grand Dame was an avid gardener and had spent the winter month's planning the layout and design of the planting bed that Lisa had unwittingly trashed.

Lisa Sutton's backside was throbbing disconcertingly while she was subjected to a most disagreeable tirade from the Grand Dame. Ms Lawton generally prided herself in delivering her most barbed scoldings in a tone of icy calm but she was so incensed that she screamed at Lisa at the top of her lungs. Lisa Sutton hung her head in shame.

The Brass and the Elite were astonished to receive an 'Eyes Only' memorandum from the Grand Dame announcing Lisa Sutton as the unit's Public Enemy Number One. The memorandum contained detailed instructions that Lisa was to be targeted as a hostile and treated with Extreme Prejudice.

It was not great time to be wearing Lisa Sutton's bumbags. Patty and her chums on the Radical Right had a field day and were all over Lisa like a rash. The unfortunate inmate could not put a foot out of place without a member of the Brass or the Elite jumping all over her bumbags. Over the next eighteen months she was punished so often that she joked that she was surprised she had not developed a permanent stoop.

Even though her status had been lowered to Public Enemy Number Two at the introduction of Operation Scorched Arse her bumbags remained classified as endangered.

Her appearances in the Grand Dame's study continued to be unpleasant and Patty and her cohorts continued to target her regularly. Without ever wittingly embarking on a campaign of mega-minxing Lisa Sutton found herself permanently ranked amongst the highest echelons of the Hall of Shame.

Lisa gasped as the whippy ashplant cruelly sliced across the sulcus at the base of her posterior. Yvonne and Janet were taking it in turns to whop Lisa and were employing the loathsome technique known as 'Low Riders'.

Predictably the technique of Low Riders was heritage Patty Hodge from her days as Red-shirt at the original Woody School. She had come across the technique in an inadvertent and painful manner during a routine caning from her House Captain. The prefect had badly miss-placed a stroke, landing it across the fleshy fold between Patty's buttocks and the tops of her thighs. It had been excruciating but Patty had been impressed by the intensity of the pain and had filed the information away for future use.

Lisa gamely remained in position, forcing herself to keep her fingers glued to her toes to avoid the evil prefects from accusing her of jerking and disqualifying the strokes.

It was tough duty and Lisa Sutton was beginning to wonder whether she might not have been better off taking her chances up in front of the Beak.

Yvonne jabbed Lisa in the chest.
"Not so cocky now, are we Sutton?' she said unpleasantly.
Lisa glared at the prefect contemptuously. She was tempted to hack Godders in the shins but didn't fancy a trip up on the stage for a public flogging. She was forced to endure another hateful diatribe from Yvonne before the thrashing was finally post-processed. She snatched back her Punishment Record Book and trudged out of the library.

14

Stalker

Janet Mitchell was beginning to feel decidedly uneasy. For the past two days everywhere she went she seemed to find Bernadette Summers leaning back against a wall, arms folded across her chest and watching her with hooded eyes.

At first Janet had merely assumed it was just coincidence but as time had worn on she began to believe that the Bounder was stalking her. Janet Mitchell was not the brightest crayon in the box but it occurred to her that Bernadette might not have approved of the prefects giving her best chum and business partner bogus whops.

Janet knew from experience that the Bounder was fiercely protective of Lisa Sutton. On several occasions Bernadette had intervened when Janet had been trying to arrange for Lisa to be dragged up to the library under a full collar. Janet Mitchell was not a brave gal by nature and had generally deferred to Bernadette's suggestions in these matters.

A Year of Sitting Painfully

"She's fucking stalking me," Janet wailed to Yvonne. "I need full time protection. You'll need to assign Ivan to act as my full-time bodyguard."

Yvonne Godfrey rolled her eyes. "Don't be such a wuss, Bitchypoo," she laughed. "You're a goddam prefect, take her to the library and give her a thrashing."

Janet stared at Yvonne gloomily. "I'm not sure she'd go for that right now."

Yvonne just shrugged and walked off.

Bernadette Summers doubled over in laughter. She had stepped out of the shadows and crept up behind Janet.

"Boo!" she had hissed in the prefect's ear. Janet Mitchell had leapt several feet in the air.

"Scared ya, didn't I?" grinned the Bounder.

"I'll get you for this," snarled Janet.

"Yeah, rock-on, Bitchypoo," drawled the Bounder and tickled her ribs with mirth.

"You're such a bad gal," giggled Lisa when Bernadette recounted Janet's recent close encounter with a heart attack.

"You should have seen her face," laughed the Bounder.

"She probably thought you were going to pop her on the hooter," grinned Lisa.

Hooter popping was playing on Janet's mind. The Bounder was notoriously unpredictable and the prefect had no doubt that Bernadette would be prepared to risk a public flogging if she felt the inclination to bop Janet on the nose. It was all most disconcerting.

Janet was deeply distressed that her cohorts on the SS were not taking her concerns seriously and offering her the appropriate protection. She had even raised the matter with Katie Beck but had received an equally unsympathetic response.

"You're a goddam Elite Gal," Katie had growled, reiterating Yvonne's opinion. "Take her up to the library and give her a thrashing."

"Grrrrrrrrr!" groaned Mitch the Bitch.

Janet was not the only one of Yvonne's cronies not having a good time of it. Juliet Spage was head down, arse up across Cathryn Cassidy's knee having her bottom spanked.

The bullying former prefect was having considerable difficulty reverting to the role of grubby. Cathryn monopolized her time having her run errands all over the compound. Cat never seemed satisfied and draped her new grubby regularly.

Juliet got no sympathy from her former SS buddies who had taken to treating her as a second-class citizen. Yvonne Godfrey had even red-carded her out of the assembly hall resulting in a most disagreeable interview with Ms Lawton.

The Radical Right was treating her badly, particularly Katie, who had given her several slipperings for clobber abuse. The unit's matron had never forgiven Juliet for trying to implicate her in her illicit spanking spree and was determined to repay her with some prime rump roastings.

Cat felt no compunction about giving Juliet frequent and extended spankings. As far as she was

A Year of Sitting Painfully

concerned Spanker was a loathsome individual and a total muff.

"Quit sniveling fool," snapped Cathryn. "All your whining gives me a headache. Now put it up and keep it up before I really get grumpy."

Juliet Spage shuffled across Cathryn's study and pressed her nose against the wall. She raised her arms and clasped her hands on her head. Tears of humiliation rolled down her cheeks.

Highly Recommended

Ms Lawton dabbed the corners of her mouth with a serviette. She had chosen to conduct her first face to face interview with Mr Humphries at a discrete Thameside restaurant. They had shared a perfectly cooked chateaubriand washed down with a bottle of 2000 Chateau Ausone Premier Grand Cru. They had chatted amiably, avoiding the subject of their meeting until after dessert.

"You have an interesting jacket, Susan," Mr Humphries said finally. "I thought the Lawton Solution was particularly inspired."

The Grand Dame looked surprised. "You have access to my military jacket?"

Mr Humphries nodded and took a sip of wine. "Yes I do," he said calmly. "I hope you don't mind but I thought it prudent to do a little research before I met you."

Susan Lawton was genuinely nonplussed. Although she had been seconded to the Ministry of Extreme Social Rehabilitation when she took over at

A Year of Sitting Painfully

the Woody Back to School unit, she remained a member of Military Intelligence and held the rank of Major. Her record was highly classified.

Susan Lawton wondered who the man seated across the table from her actually was. She had used her intelligence privileges to attempt to perform her own background check on the potential candidate to act as her successor. She had been astonished to find no records whatsoever. No national insurance number, no driving license, not even a birth certificate. She had checked the databases of several friendly international espionage agencies and had come up with nothing. It had been very frustrating.

"I also liked your school record," he continued amiably. "Quite the little minx weren't you."

Ms Lawton felt herself blushing. She had not expected the subject to come up. She was aware that to the uninformed her disciplinary record at the original Woody School might appear less than stellar.

"Although I am surprised that you chose to employ Thrasher Hodge, I can't imagine you are exactly close friends," Mr Humphries continued.

"Actually I didn't choose to employ her," said Ms Lawton quickly. "She was rather foisted on me by the System. The trouble is she's academically gifted and she had the reputation as the top disciplinarian in the country. Under the circumstances I could hardly turn down her application on the basis that she thrashed me a few times at school."

"I can see that might have been tricky," grinned Mr Humphries.

"She was an awful bitch at school and she hasn't changed one iota," said Susan. "Unfortunately at the facility she's a necessary evil, although I have to admit there are many occasions I'd like to take my cane to her backside."

"Why don't you?" asked Mr Humphries.

Ms Lawton chuckled at the thought, then glancing over at the man across the table it occurred to her that he was being entirely serious.

"Who is he?" Ms Lawton asked the Minister of Extreme Social Rehabilitation.

The Minister raised an eyebrow. "I have no idea. I thought he was one of yours. Some kind of a spook."

"He's spooky alright," said Ms Lawton, "but not the way you meant it. We don't have any record of him and nor, as far as I can tell, does anybody else."

The Minister poured the Grand Dame a glass of port. "Well he comes highly recommended."

"By whom?" asked the Grand Dame.

The Minister looked thoughtful. "Well, that's an interesting question. I'm not sure exactly. His name kept coming up and everybody always says that he comes highly recommended. I never thought to ask by whom precisely."

Ms Lawton sipped her drink. "I told you he's spooky," she said.

"But is he the right man for the job?" asked the Minister.

Ms Lawton looked the Minister straight in the eye. "I hear he comes highly recommended," she responded.

Ms Lawton leaned back in the cushioned seat of the chauffeur driven Bentley that the Minister had

A Year of Sitting Painfully

kindly requisitioned to return her to the facility. For the first time in months she felt at ease.

She felt confident that this man Humphries would be more than a match for Patty and her cronies.

She began to nod off and fell asleep with the delightful thought of taking the cane to Patricia Hodge's backside.

Hand Gabbing

Nixdown Nixon was not feeling the least bit at ease. She was standing at the front of the assembly hall seething with anger. It had taken all her resolve not to stride up to Janet Mitchell and hack her on the shins when Bitchypoo had shown her the red card.

The red card was not entirely bogus but it was marginal at best. Nixdown had merely nudged her chum Rosemary Booker and indicated to her that her tie was in an abusive condition. Janet had called her on gabbing charges which to Nicola Jane Nixon's mind was not very sporting unless sign language had suddenly been outlawed.

"This is fucking bogus," Nixdown muttered as she passed Penny Ann Evans.

"Do you want to appeal?" asked the Red-shirt.

"Yeah rock on Pen, a lot of good that would do," Nix growled and went over to stand beside the piano.

A Year of Sitting Painfully

As usual when they arrived in the hall Patty Hodge and the Wart took time out to participate in some spiteful banter.

"You're such a degenerate Nixon," said Patty. "I hope she takes the skin off your arse."

Ms Wharton cackled. Nixdown curled her lip contemptuously.

Ms Lawton swept into the hall. Immediately she caught sight of Nixdown her face hardened. She was barreling down on Nix with a face like thunder when Penelope Ann stepped forward.

"Excuse me Ma'am," said the Red-shirt politely, "but mightn't I have a word?"

Nixdown glared at Katie Beck. Katie was looking Nix up and down, hoping for an excuse to subject her to a clobber inspection. It was a fruitless task. Nicola Jane Nixon was a notorious clothes horse. Despite her contempt and disdain for the system that had incarcerated her at Woodys for a seven year sentence without the possibility of parole she took the clobber end of the whops and clobber culture very seriously.

Nixdown had availed upon her plutocratic chaps to engage a full-time Clobber Consultant to seek out new fabrics for her blazers, blouses and ties. Even the red house sash she wore knotted around her waist had been imported from a boutique factory in the Indian town of Kanchipuran. The factory only used wild-crafted silks and made Nixdown's sashes from hand-spun Tussal yarns.

"Go and bend over the desk in the ante-room," growled Katie bitterly when she came up empty. "I'll be in to inspect you shortly."

Nixdown stood facing the wall on the landing outside the Grand Dame's study. She was surprised to hear several sets of feet approaching in the corridor below. Click, click, click, clack, clack, clack. The unmistakable sound of Ms Lawton's heels in the stairwell, followed by the more subdued sound of flat soled shoes coming in her wake. Nixdown resisted the temptation to turn her face away from the wall and steadfastly maintained her pose of nose and toes as the entourage approached.

"Wait there Nixon," said Ms Lawton authoritivley, "You too Mitchell, I'll speak to you first Evans."

Nixdown heard the door of the Grand Dame's study close and could sense Janet Mitchell stepping up behind her.

Mitch the Bitch took a bunch of Nixdown's hair in her hand and twisted viciously.

"You try to make trouble for me Nixon and we'll be all over your bumbags like a rash," she snarled.

Nicola Jane kicked back, the heel of her right heel hitting Janet in the center of her shin bone.

Janet released her grip on Nix's hair and jumped back squealing. "You fucking bitch," she yelped.

Nixdown continued to stare at the wall. Katie stared down at her desktop and shuffled some paperwork.

A Year of Sitting Painfully

Behind them the door opened. "The Grand Dame would like to speak with you now, Nixon," said Penny Ann. The Red-shirt squinted. "Are you okay Janet?" she asked. "Something wrong with your leg?" Janet Mitchell just groaned and continued to rub her shin feverishly.

Nixdown shrugged and stepped through the open doorway.

"I am going to ask you to be truthful, Nixon," said the Grand Dame. "Penelope Ann Evans has made the unusual step of speaking up on your behalf. She tells me that there may have been a misunderstanding over whether you were actually gabbing. Was there a misunderstanding Miss Nixon?"

Nixdown opened her mouth to respond, but Ms Lawton held up her hand.

"Please be truthful with me Miss Nixon," she said. "Untruthfulness is a most an undesirable trait don't you think? And please be assured that if I find you to be untruthful I shall have no qualms about taking you back to the hall and giving you a most disagreeable public flogging. Now Miss Nixon, answer the question. Were you actually gabbing or was there some misunderstanding?"

"Well if we're being completely accurate Ma'am," said Nix. "Not actually gabbing but I did hand-gab."

17

Nixdown and Penelope Ann

"She pulled the strokes," Nixdown smiled. She was slowly backing Penny Ann Evans up against the wall of the stable, her fingers gently caressing the Red-shirt's cheeks.

"Nix?" Penny said uncertainly.

Nicola Jane put her fingers to her lips and hushed Penny Ann. She reached out and began to unfasten the buttons down the front of Pen's tailored hacking jacket. "Just relax and let me show you my appreciation," breathed Nix.

Penny Ann's head was spinning. She had known Nicola Jane Nixon for over a decade. They had ridden on the same circuit, coming together with Jojo and Claire Brooks to formulate the heart of the nation's riding squad and tipped for honors at the forthcoming Olympics. All that had come to nothing as the System had cynically picked them off, one by one, and had them incarcerated at the Big House.

Penelope Ann had always admired Nicola Jane. They were a study of contrasts. Nix wild and

A Year of Sitting Painfully

notoriously promiscuous, Penny Ann the quintessential English rose, shy and reserved.

Penny Ann knew of Nixdown's reputation for bedding down members of the Elite. She was aware that Nicola Jane occasionally indulged in a ménage à trois with the Amazonian Rastafarian Butcher Twins and that she also had occasional trysts with Melanie White and her gargantuan gazonkas. Penelope Ann often day-dreamed about her equestrian team-mate but was far too shy to make her feelings known. When she found herself alone with Nixdown she always managed to keep the subject matter on upcoming events and the well-being of their beloved horses.

Nixdown unknotted Penny Ann's tie and began to unbutton the front of her blouse. Being almost six inches shorter than the Red-shirt Nixdown had to tip-toe up to gently run the tip of her tongue along the line of Pen's lips. Penelope Ann Evans felt like she had died and gone to heaven.

"I need you to thrash me," breathed Nixdown. "Put me over your knee and whip me with your riding crop."

Penny Ann's eyes danced with confusion. "I don't understand," she gasped.

"Don't ask questions, just straighten yourself up and do as I ask," whispered Nix. "We can talk later."

In many ways Nicola Jane Nixon was an odd fish. Out of the Famous Four she had had the most difficulty adjusting to the austere regime of the Back to School facility. She was belligerent and defiant by nature and hated the concept that she could be beaten by the Brass and the Elite.

Her school career had been tempestuous. Her willfulness had earned her numerous canings and she had been expelled from two academies for retaliating by hacking the Headmistresses in the shins.

At the last school she attended the zealous Headmistress had hoped to curb Nix's belligerence by caning her in front of the assembled school. Nicola Jane had responded by fire-bombing her car and ended her academic career in reform school.

She had followed her auteur father into the world of video and film, carving out a reputation for making risqué music videos.

Nicola Jane became involved in a lusty affair with a cameraman. One night she was late for dinner and kept him waiting for an hour. When they returned to his apartment he had turned her over his knee and given her a blistering spanking. Predictably when she was released she had slapped his face and hacked him on the shins with her pointed boots. She had stormed out of the apartment.

Later at home, alone in bed she had found herself curiously aroused. Eventually she had slid out from under the sheets and returned to the cameraman's apartment and demanded that he Rodger her eyes out.

Nicola Jane's videos had an increasingly BDSM theme to them and she often featured herself being spanked and caned.

A Year of Sitting Painfully

Nonetheless when she was finally sentenced to the Big House she found nothing titillating about the regime. She had the misfortune to be allocated to act as Katie Beck's personal grubby and spent most of the year head down, arse up across the vicious Red-shirt's lap. It was a war of attrition; Katie spanked her and Nix hacked the Red-shirt's shins. Katie spanked her some more and would often illegally yank down her knickers earning her the nickname of Nixdown Nixon.

Nixdown hated being formally punished but she still had a penchant for pain. She sought out members of the Elite who had the benefit of private study's and access to canes. She boffed them royally in return for getting their kicks on Nix Sixty-six.

Nixdown planted a kiss on Penny Ann's lips. "See that wasn't so bad, was it?" she asked with a twinkle in her eye.

Penelope Ann smoothed down her jacket and straightened her tie. "I must be fucking barking," she sighed.

"Oh hush," laughed Nicola Jane. "As long as you're Nixdown kinda barking you can't go wrong."

Melons

Deborah Morton was bent over the end of her bed, a pillow under her tummy and her thin pajamas stretched tight across her buttocks. Her stomach was filled with butterflies and a thin bead of perspiration had formed on her brow.

Across the room Melanie White slashed her ashplant through the air, slicing it across the crown of Rosemary Booker's voluptuous rear end.

Melanie climbed the back stairs that led to the Phase Five landing and opened the door. To her surprise she found Patty Hodge standing outside the door of one of the study's.

"Where have you been?" Patty snapped.

"I've been patrolling the landings," said Melanie impatiently, "where do you think I've been?"

Patty glared at Melanie but elected to let the Dorm Raider's insolent tone pass.

"Well hurry up," said Patty. "I caught Booker and Morton gabbing after lockdown. They're already bending over."

A Year of Sitting Painfully

Melanie White took off her blazer and hung it on the back of the study door. She unfastened her cuffs and rolled back her sleeves and then loosened her collar and tie. She retrieved her ashplant and walked across the room to where Rosemary was stretched out across her bed.

Melanie set herself up and tapped the ashplant down once, twice and then thrice before swiping it through the air with considerable force.

With Patty watching her closely Melanie White had no choice but to lay it on thick.

Melanie White was a popular member of the Elite. She held the joint rank of Deputy Red-shirt and Dorm Raider. She was highly respected for the even-handed manner with which she conducted herself and for her opposition to Yvonne and her cronies.

Melanie White had grown up in the same town as Cathryn Cassidy and they had schooled together. As teenagers they had made headlines as hard core Ladettes. Nightclubs all over the country ignored the under-age laws and invited them to host lucrative Ladette parties.

Although she only stood five feet on tip-toes and had a slender waist and pert behind Melanie White possessed the most remarkable pair of mammary glands. Her gargantuan gazonkas earned her the nickname of Melons in the national press.

At school at Dartington Manor they were considered wild and rebellious which meant that they had many confrontations with the Mistress in Charge of Discipline. A role performed by none other than Miss Patricia Hodge. They were thrashed frequently.

Upon leaving school they continued to tear up the town. Cat had decided to spend a gap year working as an intern in her father's recording studio. Melons was accepted at Camford to study medicine. She was determined to follow in her father's footsteps as an internationally renowned heart surgeon.

Anti-Ladette propaganda was at its zenith. The government was desperate to distract attention from its economic follies and saw Cat and Melons as ideal targets.

After Cat was arrested and sentenced to seven years at the Big House Melanie and Cathryn's family embarked on an extensive 'Free Cat' campaign. Melanie's close friends counseled her to be cautious as the Dark Agents of the System were lurking furtively in the shadows.

For several months Melons sensibly remained on the university campus which was off-limits to the Dark Agents. However, in an unguarded moment she agreed to act as a hostess to a 'Free Cat' rave. A photograph of her dancing on a table and showing off her crown jewels appeared on the front-pages of numerous rags. She was immediately arrested and charged with Extreme Ladetting. She would start her sentence the same day as her dear chum Cat.

Undaunted by the harshness of their sentences Cat and Melons joined up with another celebrity Ladette, April Turner, who had already served her first year. They were old friends and together they would form the vanguard of mega-minxdom.

Melanie swiped the fifth stroke down and then adjusted her stance. She took her time, allowing Rosemary to settle down and then swiped the

A Year of Sitting Painfully

ashplant diagonally across the previous stripes producing a perfect five bar gate. Even the generally insouciant Rosemary wriggled and squirmed as the effects of the final stroke reverberated through her central nervous system.

Not a Good Time for Six

Deborah listened to Melanie's rubber-soled shoes approaching. She clenched her fists and gritted her teeth. Deborah Morton was acutely aware that this was not a good time to be getting ready for six.

It was less than eight hours since Reed the Weed had shown Debs a red-card and evicted her from a maths tutorial. There was no question that the card was totally justifiable but that was little consolation to Debs as she trudged through the labyrinth of corridors that led to the Grand Dame's study.

Deborah's relationship with Ms Lawton was at an all-time low. Months earlier the Grand Dame had informed Debs that whenever she was sent to her study she would receive twelve strokes of the cane until her behavior showed a marked improvement. Apparently the required improvement had yet to transpire.

A Year of Sitting Painfully

Prior to being thrashed, Deborah was forced to endure a scathing scolding which had been disagreeable in the extreme. By the time she shrugged off her blazer and bent over the back of the straight-backed chair Deborah Morton was feeling thoroughly trashed.

Deborah felt the ashplant tapping down as Melanie took her measure. She squeezed her eyes closed tightly.

During her years at the facility Deborah had been caned by innumerable members of the Elite. They had demonstrated a wide range of competencies with the short whippy ashplants that they carried but none of them had ever shown such a consummate artistry as Melanie White.

Deborah had already had two previous experiences of bending over her bed to be beaten by Melanie and they had both been particularly hot and sweaty. On neither of those occasions was she wearing a dozen stripes under her jimjams. Deborah Morton rather fancied she was about to discover a new definition of hot and sweaty.

Melanie White had a good solid stance. Her feet were solidly planted and her shoulders square. She only raised the ashplant fifteen inches above her target but she knew that was more than adequate. She swept the cane downwards, snapping her wrist at the last moment. The whippy stick landed with a formidable thwack.

Deborah's face contorted into a silent howl, her fists pummeled the duvet and her ankles twitched as the pain imploded through her already tender rump. The pain was excruciating and she knew that she had five more swipes to come.

Patty watched with a deep sense of satisfaction. Deborah's involuntary spastic reaction was extremely gratifying. Although she would have preferred to be personally delivering the whops, witnessing them was the next best thing. She was extremely impressed with Melanie's technique. Patty grinned to herself as Melons sliced the cane down for a second time.

It was not the first time in Deborah's life that she had found herself subjected to extended benders; nonetheless this unscheduled late night thrashing was causing her considerable consternation.

"It's only whops," she repeated over and over in her head. "It's only goddam whops!"

Melanie took Deborah's punishment record book and opened it. She turned to the latest page.

"Aw man," she gasped. "I didn't know. Jeez, that must have been hot. I'm so, so sorry."

Debs grimaced. "What were you gonna do? Pull the strokes with Patty standing right behind you? It wasn't your fault."

As usual Dorm Beatings were processed the following morning just before brekker. Debs and Rosemary had cut along to Melanie's study to have their records updated.

A Year of Sitting Painfully

Melanie hugged Debs. "I know but I still feel terrible."

Debs hugged Melons back. "I'll live," she said tightly, "But I gotta tell ya sister I did not get a lot of sleep last night. You are one big whopper!"

Melons grinned. "Well there are only a couple of weeks left before furlough. Try and keep your nose clean and look forward to enjoying a cool-arse summer."

"Hallelujah to that, sister," groaned Deborah whole-heartedly.

A Painful Journey

Deborah placed her duffel bag and tennis racquets in the trunk of her mother's car. Debs had been granted a weekend pass to play in a prestigious amateur tennis tournament in the north of the country. Unusually Ms Lummell, who acted as her coach, was unavailable to accompany her. To comply with the supervisory rules of her sentence Ma Morton had volunteered to stand in.

Ma Morton was chatting with Jane Lummell getting some last minute instructions. Debs was getting antsy. She wanted to put some distance between her bumbags and the canes at the facility for a couple of much needed cool-arse days.

"I'm sorry, Morton," said Jennifer Gardiner in a low voice, "but I have to give you this."

Debs gaped at the grubby as she shoved a red envelope into her hand.

"Evans is waiting for you in the library," said Jen and hurried off.

A Year of Sitting Painfully

Deborah's mind was racing. Glancing around the parking lot she saw Yvonne and Janet. They were watching her with fish-eating smirks on their faces.

"Grrrrrrrrrrrrrrrrrrr!" muttered Debs. She hurried over to her mother.

"I'll be right back," she said as cheerfully as she could muster. "I left something upstairs."

Her mother just shrugged and carried on chatting.

Deborah hurried through the corridors, taking the stairs two at a time. She speed-walked down the landing leading to the library and burst through the door.

Penelope Ann Evans was waiting for her. "Look Debs, I don't like this any more than you do," the Red-shirt started to say. "If you want to appeal I'll support you."

Debs shrugged off her blazer as she hurried down the library. "There's no time for that Evans," she said, tossing her jacket to one side. "We need to get this over as quickly as possible." She grabbed the spanking stool and placed it in front of the fireplace. "Hurry up Evans, we haven't got all day."

Deborah was seething. She knew that Yvonne and Janet had stitched her up like a kipper. Somehow they must have learned that Ma was picking her up so they had left issuing the fateful fifth black mark until the last minute. They had probably guessed that Debs wouldn't wish to enter into the protracted appeal process with her mother waiting outside in the car-park.

They had banked on the fact that she would be forced to allow herself to be subjected to a totally bogus dangling. It made her blood boil.

Under normal circumstances danglings were drawn out affairs. However Penny Ann gathered from Deborah's desperate sense of urgency that the circumstances were not normal. She flipped back Deborah's skirt and quickly rolled down her bumbags. She raised the ceremonial hairbrush in the air and slammed it down.

Deborah writhed and kicked her legs. She pummeled the air with her fists and shook her head from side to side. The blistering salvo was absolutely excruciating. Penny Ann was working quickly and the whole affair took barely thirty seconds.

Deborah slid off Penny Ann's lap, grabbing under her skirt to straighten her bumbags. She felt quite giddy and her backside was roaring like a furnace. She limped over to where her discarded blazer had landed and reached for her Punishment Record Book.

Penny Ann wrote as quickly as possible. Debs was replacing her blazer and rubbing her eyes on the sleeve.

"Are you okay?" asked Penny Ann.

Deborah pursed her lips and nodded. She grabbed the book out of the Red-shirts hand and hurried out of the library.

"I'm sorry about that, Ma," panted Debs.

"Are you alright, Deborah?" asked her mother. "You look a little flushed."

A Year of Sitting Painfully

"I'm fine, Ma," Debs lied. "We should get going; I don't want to be late for registration for the tournament."

Ma Morton said her goodbyes to Ms Lummell and opened the door to the driver's seat. "Are you going to drive?" she asked Debs.

"No, Ma. You drive," mumbled Deborah. "If you don't mind I'd like to sit in the back and take a nap. You're right I'm not feeling too good, I've got a splitting headache."

Her mother nodded sympathetically.

Deborah slid painfully into the back seat. Across the car park she caught Yvonne and Janet's eyes. They waved at her gleefully. Deborah Morton shot them the bird and settled in for a long painful journey.

The Dirty Dozen

As year drew to an end and the summer furlough approached the Dirty Dozen were being whopped at record breaking rates.

When Ms Lawton had first announced the implementation of Operation Scorched Arse she had provided the Brass and Elite with a list of twelve inmates that she predicted would be the most disruptive. She branded them the Dirty Dozen. Her prediction had proved to be unerringly accurate. The twelve inmates she had selected resided in the top positions on the Annual Hall of Shame.

Every one of them had been caned over thirty times and four of them had passed the forty mark. Lisa Sutton and Cassandra Cassidy were at forty one and forty two respectively. Debs was ranked at number two with forty-five lickings under her bumbags and Jojo led the pack with forty-nine and seemed destined to score her second consecutive Bull before the year was out.

Lady Victoria Brompton and Claire Brooks had established records for inmates being punished during

A Year of Sitting Painfully

the sixth year of their sentence. Cathryn Cassidy had become the most caned prefect in history, followed closely by her partner in crime Melanie White.

It was a joyous time to be a member of the Radical Right or a Serial Spanker. Despite Ms Lawton's efforts to restrain them the misbehavior of the mega-minxes gave them abundant opportunities to rattle rattan across tautened gossamer.

Patty, Katie and the Wart spent their evenings propping up the bar at the Bunch of Grapes and regaling each other with their recent successes.

Yvonne, Janet, Ivan and Jayne Underly continued to manipulate the system to score copious supplies of whops.

The lecture rooms and corridors echoed with the sound of canes, straps and slippers rebounding from upturned derrieres.

Deborah Morton looked gloomily at the standings on the Hall of Shame. She was highly competitive by nature and it astonished her that she found herself once again playing second fiddle to Jojo Heyworth.

In her unfortunate position as Public Enemy Number One and Ms Lawton's personal bête noire it had been a busy year inside Deborah's bumbags by any standards. However, with only ten days left of the year she was four lickings behind her good chum and had little chance of catching up.

When she had first embraced the lifestyle of mega-minxdom Debs had naturally presumed that she would eventually assume the mantle of Big BUTT. It was not a particularly outlandish assumption.

During the five years she had spent at the ultra-strict Queensgate Academy she had received the cane on more occasions than any other school pupil in recorded history. The Ministry of Education records date back to the early eighteen fifties.

During her first year at the facility she had been spanked liberally and had even received the cane from the Grand Dame. Nonetheless, Jojo had trumped her on both counts, receiving several more spankings and being caned twice.

Over the next few years Debs and Jojo had whopped it out on the Hall of Shame but somehow Jojo always managed to stay ahead. During the second, third, and fourth years of her sentence Joanna Heyworth had earned the title of Annual Big BUTT. During their fourth year at the facility Deborah had watched jealously as Jojo became the first inmate in the facility's history to score a Bull, accumulating fifty whoppings in a single year.

Staring at the current standings Deborah Morton figured she was destined to always be the bridesmaid but never the bride.

Jojo stared at the ranking on the Hall of Shame with considerable satisfaction. It was inconceivable that with ten days still remaining before the unit broke for summer furlough that she wouldn't score a second consecutive Bull. Throughout the year she had executed a perfect campaign of Extreme Minxing. Without attracting the type of animosity that Deborah frequently inspired, Jojo's sustained program of larking, pranking, goofing and gabbing had paid dividends. Jojo was rightfully proud of her record.

A Year of Sitting Painfully

Cassie Cassy was also justifiably proud of her record. She had never made any secret of the fact that she aspired to eventually rise to the position of All-Time Big BUTT. Finding herself in third position behind such legendary über-minxes as Jojo and Debs was deeply satisfying. With four years still left to serve of her sentence Cassandra Cassidy had her eye firmly fixed on the title.

A Wriggler and a Giggler

Cassie Cassy shrugged off her red and black striped blazer and hung it over the back of the chair. She looked over at the English Dame with a slightly demented expression on her face.

"Bend over the desk," instructed Ms Powell.

"Yes Ma'am," said Cassie and then she began to giggle.

Stephanie Powell shook her head in bewilderment. Like the other Dames at the facility she had become accustomed to Cassie's unusual reaction to being informed that she was about to be beaten. Cassie claimed that it was a nervous affliction, but it was the general consensus that it was merely another indication that she was certifiably barking.

Cassie Cassy was the antithesis of her ultra-cool sister, Cathryn. Whereas Cat always seemed calm and collected Cassie was exuberant, effervescent and scatter-brained.

Cassie was an extraordinary looking creature. She had inherited her super-model mother's looks, sparkling blue eyes, a mane of blonde hair, and the

A Year of Sitting Painfully

smile of an angel. Nonetheless she was an angel with an extremely dirty face. As best as anybody could tell all that Cassie ever took seriously was cooking and minxing.

Cassie slid her upper torso across the desk-lid. She stretched out her arms and reached over to grip the legs on the far side. When Ms Powell folded Cassie's skirt back her victim emitted another giggle.

Stephanie Powell flexed the thirty-inch long number one cane between her hands and focused her attention on her navy blue clad target. The English Dame was fond of Cassandra and bore her no harm. However, she was duty bound to give Cassie a good, tight licking so she raised her arm in the air and brought it down swiping.

Cassie was a wriggler. She was a die-hard believer in the minx mantra that only muffs howl, but nonetheless she liked to allow herself a wriggle and squirm between strokes.
"It helps me set up and focus for the next one," she was fond of telling anybody who was willing to listen.

Stephanie Powell took her time and allowed Cassie to wriggle her butt a bit and then settle down before setting up for the next stroke. Caning Cassie was a stress free project. Ms Powell knew that after some momentary wiggling and jiggling Cassandra Cassidy was guaranteed to put it up and keep it up.

Cassie pushed her buttocks up, offering the Dame the optimum target. On the rare occasions that she had given it any thought Cassie Cassy had concluded that she didn't much care for being caned but was resigned to it being a bi-product of her chosen lifestyle. She had also concluded that putting it up fair and square gave her disciplinarian the greatest chance of hitting the sweet spot and limited the potential for painful low-riders or wraparounds. Everything was a trade-off Cassie Cassy told herself.

Ms Powell warmed to her work, slicing and dicing Cassie Cassy's bumbags with consummate precision.
She landed six clean stripes in tight formation. She watched Cassie wriggle and squirm as the last stroke ripped home. A job well done, Stephanie thought to herself.

Cassie Cassy unfolded herself from the desk and retrieved her blazer from the back of her chair. She shrugged it on, flicked her hair back and fastened the top button. She followed Ms Powell to the front of the lecture room.
Cassie reached into the breast pocket of her blazer and pulled out her well-worn personal punishment record book and handed it to the Dame. When Ms Powell began to annotate the PRB with Cassie's latest misadventure with the cane Cassandra began to giggle.

"You're certifiably barking, you know, don't you?" laughed Jojo.

A Year of Sitting Painfully

Cassie was lying across the lap of her mentor and idol having her weals soothed with mystical balms.

Cassie just wriggled and giggled.

Miss Claire Brooks

Claire Brooks wasn't giggling. Mdme Diderot had taken a hold of the knot of her tie and yanked her out of her seat. The French Dame had pulled Claire forward until their faces were only inches apart. Apart from having to gasp for breath Claire was confronted with the full force of Mdme's Gauloisse and absinthe halitosis and the pungent cloud created by her over-powering bordello scent.

"It was just a joke Mademoiselle," Claire spluttered helplessly.

"A joke? Just a joke?" roared the French Dame. "I shall show you a joke Mademoiselle Brooks," and thrust Claire downwards across her desk. "Ha very ha!" she gloated as she yanked Claire's skirt back.

"Ha!" she seethed as she slashed the cane downwards. "Ha and Ha and Ha and Ha!" The French Dame was caning fast, the five strokes landing in a flurry. Claire hardly had time to catch her breath between the swipes. Mdme Diderot finally stepped back, flexing her cane and preparing to bring the thrashing to its conclusion.

A Year of Sitting Painfully

Claire's chums watched with sympathetic detachment. The sight of Claire being yanked out of her seat by irate dames was not uncommon.

On first impressions Claire Brooks seemed an unlikely candidate for mega-minx stardom. She was quietly spoken and seemed to have impeccable manners. She gave the impression of being very reserved. People also noticed how remarkably neat she always looked. Her blouses seemed whiter than white and never appeared crumpled even towards the end of the day. Her tie was always perfectly knotted and her shoes shone brightly. Claire Brooks was quite the dandy and held a unique Woody record as the only inmate never to have been slippered by Katie for clobber abuse.

Nonetheless, still waters run deep and her chums knew another side of her. Claire Brooks was a natural comedienne and possessed a lightening wit. Unfortunately for Claire she had a habit of wagging her chin before engaging her brain. Her chums found her humorous interjections into dry lecture proceedings hilarious, unfortunately the Dames did not always appreciate Claire's penchant for pith.

It was not just the Dames at Woodys who had taken exception to Claire's jocularity. At boarding school she had quickly established a reputation as the classroom comic and spent many hours in the detention room writing boring lines and impositions.

Finally she was summonsed before the Head Prefect who was concerned about the frequency with which Claire appeared in the detention room.

"I think we'd better try a swishing don't you?" she had asked rather dryly.

Claire Brooks did not find the proposition in the least bit unreasonable. For several years her pithy rejoinders had resulted in blistering attacks on her rear end with Ma Brooks' infamous hairbrush. She calmly bent over the arm of the House Captain's sofa.

For the next five years a wide variety of prefects, Headgirls and members of the teaching staff would try out the cane on Claire's arse in vain attempts to teach her to curb her motor-mouth.

As she grew older her vocabulary became more colorful and her ripostes more ribald. At sixteen years old and over fifty canings into her career she was eventually expelled after she was discovered in a compromising position with a healthy stable-boy.

Mdme Diderot was a queer fish. She was once young, beautiful and married. However her taste for absinthe had dissipated her good looks and her husband had abandoned her. She had taken tutoring assignments across the Channel and had been surprised to find the cane still in use. Corporal punishment had been abolished in the French school system a century and a half before.

Although she was not a whop junkie on the scale of Patty or the Wart she saw the value in delivering a sore bottom as a means of retribution for disorderly behavior.

She was a solitary cove. She was aligned with neither the Radical Right nor the Liberal Left. She spent her evenings locked in her quarters drinking absinthe, chain-smoking Gauloisse's and listening to endless recordings of Maria Callas.

She was not well-known for her sense of humor and shared none of the enlightened philosophies of her namesake. Mdme Diderot did not find Claire Brooks in the least bit amusing. She took a tight grip on the cane and raised it high in the air.

"She's such a crabby bitch," grumbled Claire to Lady Vix. "She's got no sense of humor."
Victoria laughed. "She's French, what do you expect?" she asked.
"Well, there is always that," acknowledged Claire.

Bad Times for Spanker Spage

Spanker Spage was not amused; in fact she was blubbing like a muff. She was standing before the Grand Dame with her head bowed and tears running freely down her cheeks.

"You are our first failure, Spage," Ms Lawton was telling her. "Over the past ten years I have been responsible for rehabilitating the worst examples of Ladette culture and our program has been an unmitigated success. However, it must be expected that there will always be one rotten apple in every barrel and you Spage are rotten to the core."

Juliet Spage's shoulders pulsated as she sobbed. "It wasn't my fault," she spluttered. "They made me do it."

"Oh put a sock in it Spage," snapped Ms Lawton. "You attempted to mace Cassidy and now you're trying to blame others? You are completely beyond redemption Spage."

Cathryn Cassidy took off her blazer and rolled up her sleeves. She loosened her tie and spat on her

A Year of Sitting Painfully

hands. "Come here Spage," she said, sitting down on an armless chair.

Spanker Spage glared at her Personal Draper hatefully. The past six months had been a nightmare for the former member of the SS. Ever since Juliet had been kicked out of the Elite, and reduced to the role of a grubby, life had been tough. Every waking hour that Spanker was not attending lectures or in the study hall Cathryn kept her busy.

The other grubby's had benefited greatly from Juliet's reduced circumstances. When Cathryn ran out of errands for Juliet to run she loaned her out to other members of the Elite. Melons, Penny Ann and the Butcher Twins were more than happy to have Juliet relieve their own personal grubbys from duty as they put Spanker to work.

Spanker's former cohorts from the SS had not proven to be a loyal bunch. They regularly mocked her when they came across her on the Elite landing. Yvonne Godfrey had even taken the opportunity to red card Juliet out of the assembly hall on two occasions causing her to receive twelve stroke bare benders from the Grand Dame.

Her former handler, Katie Beck, monitored Juliet's laundry vigilantly and slippered her on marginal charges of clobber abuse.

The Wart targeted her ruthlessly during tutorials and alternated between beating her locally and red-carding her up to Ms Lawton's office.

It was a miserable time for the once powerful Brat Draper and the worst of it was she had to contend with her most hated enemy, Cathryn Cassidy.

Cat had always been the most strident opponent of the Secret Sorority of Serial Spankers. Yvonne and her cronies had made it a policy to give Cat a wide berth whenever possible and wisely Spanker had never included Cat's personal grubby in her serial spanking activities.

To be subjected to the ignominy of being forced to act as Cathryn Cassidy's personal grubby was almost too much for Juliet to bear.

Juliet Spage was quite surprised when Yvonne Godfrey sidled up and started making all nice to her. The Commandant of the SS started by inviting her former aide down to one of her stash areas and plying her with booze and cigarettes. Yvonne made sympathetic noises about Juliet's plight, even apologizing for red-carding her.

"It was all for the cause," she explained. "Ms Lawton has us under ob's and I needed to show her we weren't cutting you any slack."

Juliet grunted. She had known Yvonne a long time and knew only too well that she didn't have a sympathetic bone in her body.

"You want something, don't you?" she demanded.

Yvonne shrugged. "I need a favor," she admitted. "That bitch Cassidy got me a whopping and she's gonna pay for it! You'd love to see Cassidy get her comeuppance, now wouldn't you my dear Spanker."

Spanker Spage looked suspicious. "What do you want me to do?"

Yvonne reached into her pocket and extracted a small canister. "This is mace," she told her former

A Year of Sitting Painfully

chum. "I want you to pitch up late for grubbing duties. Cassidy will be obliged to drape you. Just act normal and then when you're in close spray this in her eyes. I'll be waiting on the landing with Ivan. When she goes down we'll come in and throw a sack over her head and wrap her up with duct tape. We'll shove her in the closet for a few hours and then after lock-down we'll sneak her over to the stables and thrash the shit out of her."

"Oh good grief," was all Spanker could think of to say.

Sniff Test

Yvonne's assessment that Cathryn had been responsible for the disagreeable twelve stroke whopping she had received from Patty Hodge was not entirely accurate.

As usual Yvonne had been acting the bollocks. She had been swaggering around the recreation area with her pack of cohorts looking for opportunities to score some cheap whops.

Cathryn Cassidy was the day's nominated duty monitor and was positioned on the landing of the ornate stairway that led to the Main House. It gave her a perfect vantage point to observe all the areas of the recreation ground including the cloisters and the quadrangle. It was a warm day and most of the inmates were taking advantage of the good weather to get some fresh air. They were congregated in small pockets playing a variety of card games or backgammon or just plain kicking back and gabbing.

Cathryn spotted Yvonne and her chums swanking about the place. She sighed and made her way down the stairwell.

A Year of Sitting Painfully

"What are you up to Godders?" she asked when she caught up with the SS. "I don't need any assistance and especially not from you."

"Oh put your fucking bumbags in it Cassidy," replied Yvonne. "We're just taking a stroll. We've got just as much right to the rec area as anybody else."

"Well don't start acting the bollocks on my watch," said Cat threateningly, "I'll be watching you."

Yvonne just sneered. Cat returned to her lookout post, keeping a careful eye on the members of the SS.

Cat yawned and looked at her watch. She dearly wished that she could take a nap. The previous evening after the facility had been put under lockdown she had shimmied down a drainpipe and sneaked across the grounds. She had climbed over the wall of the orchard and into the arms of her boyfriend Mark who was waiting in his car.

Cat and Mark had met in a coffee shop in the nearby town and had been going hot and heavy ever since. Cat regularly broke out of the unit at night so that she could spend some quality time with her beau.

Her late night trysts had gone undiscovered but her relationship had nonetheless not been altogether beneficial to her bumbags. On several occasions she had missed curfews and been caned by the Duty Dames. On the third occasion Patty had insisted that she was paraded in front of the Beak and Ms Lawton had given her a severe scolding and a twelve-stroke bare bender. It had little effect and several weeks later when she cut curfew again

Cathryn Cassidy became the first prefect in Woody history to be publicly flogged.

Cathryn continued to yawn. She hated being duty monitor. It was such a drag. She always did her best to cut the inmates as much slack as possible but during free-time, away from the strict discipline of the lecture rooms and study groups, they were always at their most rambunctious. It was a rare day that the duty monitor wasn't obliged to take at least one inmate up to the library for a thrashing.

Cat watched Yvonne sauntering about, she and her cronies stopped several times at groups of inmates. Cathryn had little doubt that they were making snide comments and underlying threats but at least they moved on.

Cat looked at her watch again. Six-twenty. In the distance, several stragglers were ambling along the driveway, back from excursions into town, just in time for Callover. Below in the recreation areas the inmates were packing up their belongings and preparing to go back to the main building. Cat Cassidy wandered down the steps. It wouldn't be long now, she figured, before she could cut along to her study and enjoy a much-needed power-nap.

Cathryn crossed the recreation area and followed the inmates into the building. They were making their way up the stairwells towards the landings so that they could put their kit away. She headed towards the assembly hall to help Penelope Ann oversee Callover.

A Year of Sitting Painfully

"What the fuck are you doing?" growled Cathryn.

She had turned into a corridor and encountered Yvonne backing Rosemary up against a wall.

"She's been smoking," said Yvonne, "I can smell it on her breath. I'm searching her."

Cathryn narrowed her eyes. "Did you find anything?"

Yvonne cut her eyes at Cat. "Mind your own business, Cassidy, I haven't finished," she snarled. "Raise your skirt," she instructed Rosemary.

Rosemary Booker took the hem of her skirt and raised it. Yvonne reached over and ran her fingers around the waistband of Rosemary's bumbags working front to back.

She reddened slightly when she came up empty. "I can still smell it on her breath," she said defiantly.

"Yeah rock on, Godders," said Cathryn Cassidy. "Come here Rosemary; let's see if you pass a sniff test."

26

The Sacking of Spanker Spage

Patty Hodge's olfactory senses were legendary and she claimed that she could smell fag-breath at twenty paces. Patty was a smoking hypocrite. For thirty years she had been an on-again, off-again smoker and alternated between being an anti-fag zealot and defending her three-pack a day habit. She hadn't smoked a cigarette for almost a week.

"Breathe out," she instructed Rosemary.

"Bend over the desk you fucking imbecile," Patty screeched into Yvonne's face. "What were you thinking?"

"She's on your fucking hit-list," Yvonne screamed back. "You're not whopping me for this!"

Patty stared at Yvonne. "You can bet your bottom dollar I'm whopping you for this. It's reckless behavior like this that gets the SS a bad name. You're lucky I don't bring you up in front of an SS hearing and have you stripped of your rank as Commandant. Now bend over the desk before I summons Ivan to hold you down."

A Year of Sitting Painfully

"You are a truly rotten bitch, Patty," said Yvonne through gritted teeth and then slowly she peeled off her blazer.

The macing had not gone well. As she had approached Cathryn Juliet had reached into her blazer pocket intending to palm the small canister. As sleight of hand went it had been particularly guileless and Cat had caught on fast. She leapt out of the seat and slapped Juliet's hand aside, at the same time she stamped her right foot down on top of Juliet's causing Spanker to roar out and take a tumble.

"What the fuck is this?" asked Cat, retrieving the canister from the floor. "Mace? You were going to fucking mace me? Oh you pathetic bitch," she growled and toed Spanker in the ribs with the sharp point of her shoe. "Get up you little weasel, I rather fancy you won't be sitting down again this week."

"She tried to mace you," said Penelope Ann insistently. "We need to report this."

"I've taken care of her," said Cat stubbornly.

"Taken care of it?" asked Patsy Butcher incredulously. "You've spanked her. What's to stop her sneaking in and zapping you with chloroform while you're sleeping?"

"She's clearly deranged, Cat," agreed Lindsey Butcher. "We need to deal with this."

Even Melanie White nodded her consensus. "I've known you a long time Cat and I know you think you can take care of everything but this is just too far out where the buses don't run. We don't have any choice; we'll have to involve the Beak in this one."

"Hmmm," grumbled Cathryn noncommittally.

"I could flog you and flunk you," Ms Lawton told Spanker Spage. "Send you before a hearing of the System and put you back a few years to see whether we can't beat some goodwill into you, but I think not. I'm going to sack you Spage and hand you over to the constabulary. You will be charged with attempted assault and possession of a prohibited substance. I rather think that you're going to chokey Miss Spage and I for one hope that they throw away the key."

"Naaaaawwwwwww!!!!" wailed Spanker Spage.

"You really didn't have any choice," said Mr Humphries over dinner.

"It's a shame though," sighed Susan Lawton. "Ten years without a single sacking and now with just ten days to go this happens."

Mr Humphries smiled, "Well in ten days you'll start your new life," he told her cheerily, "and then it will become my problem."

"Ten days is a long time at the Woody Back to School unit," Susan sighed wearily.

www.ingramcontent.com/pod-product-compliance
Lightning Source LLC
LaVergne TN
LVHW011427080426
835512LV00005B/301